PAINTINGS AND DRAWINGS BY HANS ZANDER

Market Places

PERSONAL COMMERCE IN ONTARIO

A Prentice-Hall/Newcastle book

Dedication:
FOR JULIA

Published by:

Prentice-Hall Canada Inc.
1870 Birchmount Road
Scarborough, Ontario, M1P 2J7, Canada

Printed and bound in Canada.

CANADIAN CATALOGUING IN PUBLICATION DATA
Zander, Hans.
  Markets of Ontario

ISBN 0-13-557108-1

1. Markets — Ontario. 2. Farm produce — Ontario — Marketing. I. Title.

HF5472.C32059   381′.18′09713   C81-095058-8

Contents

Foreword

LOAVES AND FISHES, SAUSAGE AND STRAWBERRIES

ONE NIGHT not long ago I was sitting in a tavern in downtown Toronto. The band up front was hard rock, and a smallish girl of nineteen with shoulder-length, medium-blonde hair was singing while the lead guitar, bass and drums hammered along behind her strong young voice. She was always moving, partly to the beat and partly to an awareness of her own role — thrusting a fist into the air as she shouted a line to the beer drinkers stretching off into the gloom, turning her head to meet the eyes of the drummer or the bass player or the whirling dervish on lead guitar . . . and into my mind came a picture of her, the singer, my daughter, back in the mid-1960s, when no Saturday morning went by that I did not go into her room early, the rest of the house asleep, and find her sitting up in her pyjamas, not long awake. I'd say, "Ready to go to the market?" And she'd scramble to get ready.

They knew us as a couple at the market — the old St. Lawrence Market, since replaced on the same site by a new building that is remarkably faithful to the spirit of the old. I was probably known as that guy with the little girl. She liked to ride my shoulders or go piggyback as I edged through the crowds, but sometimes I would have to put her down among the forest of adult legs moving slowly along the aisles. Once she slipped free from my hand and darted away. When I found her, minutes later, she was conversing nose to nose with the severed head of a pig.

There was a big old lady, dead now, who used to sell her own homemade sausage down at the southeast corner of the market. She would look at me every week, and then look down to where my daughter's eyes barely cleared the wooden plank that formed a countertop. Gravely the old lady would cut a small slice from a sausage end for me, and then say to my daughter, "You like?" Then she would slice her a piece as well. I remember that sausage today, two kinds, one with garlic. I would always buy both kinds, and they would be wrapped and put in my shopping bag. We would go on to buy or not to buy, depending on whether the black radishes here were a little cheaper than the ones there, or whether this bread or that pickle looked worth a try.

I remember especially one Christmas Eve when I couldn't find a turkey I liked, and went home to be told the stores were all sold out of the frozen ones. I sped back to the market. The only turkey left looked not at all like the fat and frozen packaged birds of the supermarkets. Hard bones seemed to stick out all over. But it was all there was, and the next day when it was cooked, being fresh and unfrozen, it had the best flavour I had tasted in a turkey since I was a boy on the Prairies and thought all turkeys tasted like that.

But time goes on. That night when my daughter was playing the smoky tavern, I thought fleetingly of fourteen years earlier, when she'd held my hand at the market. Then I didn't think of the market again until in a room full of people a few weeks later I heard my wife say, "Scott is a market freak." She went on to tell of a nine-hour layover in Helsinki on our way to the Moscow Olympics, when we had been lucky enough to be taken (by our mildly anti-Soviet Finnish guide) to the city's famous old quayside market. I bought a folded paper cone of strawberries at a stall and strolled around the other stands eating them and seeing what was different. Some of the fish were.

"And Kiev," my wife said, to remind me.

Well, yes. We were in Kiev for a soccer game between Iraq and Greece. On the first day, the young woman in the front of the Intourist bus was pointing out places of interest. "That large building over on the left," she said, in her carrying voice, "is the farmers' market. It is open every day." I watched closely thereafter for landmarks so I would be able to find my way back. Next morning my wife and I did not go on the tour bus to see monuments and museums and such, but walked to the market in lovely summer sunshine. There I saw for the first time anywhere wild strawberries being sold in paper cups, scooped full from two-foot piles of the tiny sweet berries, the largest about the size of my smallest fingernail. I have a lot of wild strawberries on my own place in the Cavan hills near Peterborough. Sometimes to liven up a fruit salad or pie we sit down in a good patch and pick a pint in less than half an hour. But to pick them by the gallon or peck seemed to me amazing. I pictured the old Ukrainian *babushkas* crawling slowly on their knees through the wild strawberry patch until they had enough to take to market.

But, as I learned later on, the Kiev market was operating fourteen hundred years ago. With that in mind, the view becomes a little clearer. Wild strawberries, then as now, were purely country things, centuries short of being developed into the huge domestic berries of today. When a man was taking pigs or sheep or a bag of grain to market in Kiev long ago, wouldn't it be reasonable that his wife, if she were industrious, might take something of her own? And so she took the wild strawberries, to trade for cloth or something else she wanted. Such customs do not die out, even in fourteen hundred years.

In that connection, an argument can be made that what is widely conceded to be the world's oldest profession is actually no better than second; second to going to market. From our earliest recorded history, when family groups lived along water courses because water was as essential to life as fire, barter with neighbouring groups took place. As human skills advanced, the first crude money based on silver or gold began to relieve rich people, at least, of having to take a cow to market to barter for other goods. But markets existed long before the first recorded minting of coins, which was five or six centuries before the birth of Christ. Buddha was alive then, and Confucius. As H.G. Wells wrote in *The Outline of History*, when swarthy workers in the delta of the Nile were unloading stone for the latest pyramid contract, one might imagine "some hawker merchant in Egypt spreading his stock of Babylonish garments before the eyes of some pretty, rich lady." It had to be in a market.

I do not wish to offend anyone who believes differently, but I have a certain idea about the time of Christ as well. I refer you to where it says in the gospels that Christ, in the middle of the five thousand believers (or reasonable facsimiles) gathered near Bethsaida, took five barley loaves and two fishes that a boy was carrying in a basket, "and looking up to heaven . . . blessed them," whereupon the five thousand ate their fill. I am convinced that somewhere nearby (forgive me, Lord) there was a market.

In an ancient Bible that I recovered long ago while browsing through a whole gunny sack of Bibles belonging to my maternal grandmother (she was a Presbyterian minister's wife), there is a valuable reference section on objects in the Scriptures. Under "baskets," the first mentioned is a "*cophinus*, reticule or handbasket, usually carried on the arm by every Jew. It was this basket which each apostle filled with the superfluous fragments after the feeding of the five thousand." Another larger type is also mentioned: "A market basket, such as that in which the lad was hawking the barley loaves and fishes." I rest my case.

The evolution of markets since that time is more easily traceable. People always must have had fun at markets, too, because around the latter part of the eighth century, when Charlemagne was Holy Roman Emperor, he issued an edict telling poor folk not to let themselves go at fairs (a term used then for a larger, special type of market). This apparently they were prone to do, since markets were the only distraction, the sole opportunity for sociability, open to those who were slaves to the land. A few centuries later there are records of fine cloth being transported on the backs of men and beasts across Europe to the market at Novgorod, the capital of the most powerful republic in Russia. Even then, markets tended to be more or less regular. It helped the producer to know that if he took his stuff to a certain place at a certain time, he would find buyers expecting him.

The centre of the walled medieval city was almost always the principal church or cathedral. Alongside it, sometimes right against the church walls, were market stalls — located there because, as Lewis Mumford related in his book *The Culture of Cities*, "it was there that the citizens most frequently assembled," not only for religious purposes but for speeches or entertainments in the adjacent town square.

I rather hate to admit this, but it seems necessary to mention that those early marketplaces were the forerunners of today's malls and shopping centres. In the sixteenth century (Mumford again), "the public markets and producers' shops of the medieval town were being converted into specialized shops under continuous operation." But producers would always set up other open markets which functioned on special market days only, once or twice a week, the type we have in Ontario today.

In this sense, another market that I sometimes visit, the Kensington, in Toronto, spans both the old and the new modes. The bakeries and fish, meat, poultry and cheese shops are mainly indoors, while fruit and vegetables are sold from outside stands in all but the coldest weather.

The sociability of markets has survived rather well, too. At one time this was found mainly in modest taverns, but Toronto's St. Lawrence Market area has spawned several good, and often expensive, eating places. Kensington has only a few, but in these few the local market's breads, cheeses and fish — especially fish cooked and served in the Portuguese style — are reflected on the menus. The same linking of fine restaurants to the producers' stalls has happened to a certain extent around the Byward Market in Ottawa, where farmers sell bags of potatoes, onions and other vegetables straight from their truck beds to early-rising chefs.

It is sometimes hard for a wayfaring stranger to go by marketplaces without buying something, even while knowing that the managements of most major hotels frown on cooking in the rooms. This disadvantage need not be overpowering. In the market housed in and around Quebec City's old railway station, my wife and I picked up a couple of pounds of shrimp — brought in fresh every day, the man told us, from his own boats working out of Sept-Iles. A few hours later we sat on the bank of the St. Lawrence behind our tourist cabin, lighted a small hibachi, and cooked and ate shrimp until we could eat no more. It reminded me of our earlier experience in Kiev, where we had bought a few tomatoes and radishes and a cucumber and had later picked up some bread and beer. At lunchtime, we had sat on the deep outer window ledge of an old stone building at the edge of the city's main square, making sandwiches with my jackknife and drinking beer from the bottles, watching the world go by.

Perhaps it takes a certain cast of mind to head for markets in any city being visited for the first time. If so, many people have it. Such travellers know that a market will tell them more about local customs and pursuits than a hundred guided tours. In the marketplace at Folkestone in England, I learned that no other place I've ever been produced black cherries of such size and sweetness. In London, I have been at the Covent Garden Market in the morning, to see the fruit and vegetables and flowers wheeled in by the special breed of man who lives out his life there. In the fish market at London's Billingsgate, the pubs open at 2 a.m. They are supposed to serve only the workers there; in one, the publican told me I could not buy a pint because I was not a worker in the market.

"How do you know?" I asked

"Ye don't smell like one, mate," he said.

But right then three fish-gutters needed a fourth for darts. I had my darts with me and volunteered. The fish-gutters bought my pint for me. Their hands were covered with tiny cuts where their razor-sharp cleaning knives had slipped a little.

To me, the joys of markets come in two categories: the things I know, the familiar tried and true, and the unknown. The familiar rarely comes easily, but is the result of experimenting with the new. Corn on the cob for me means sampling a half-dozen here and a half-dozen there, until one variety stands out. At the St. Lawrence Market twenty years ago, I found an open-air stall where a girl in her early teens silently peeled back a husk and showed me a big cob with an uncommonly large number of rows of sweet-looking small kernals. "It's good," was all she said. It was. For years thereafter I would see her in the corn season. She reached her middle teens and her late teens and became a young woman. When I would stop at her family's stall in mid-August, she would say, before I even spoke, "Not yet. Maybe in a week or two." One day it would be there.

I have not seen her for years now, but I think of her from time to time. She would be in her thirties now. I think of her as married, with children who may or may not live out their childhoods like hers. She used to get up at three each Saturday morning (she told me once) to help pack corn into gunny sacks, then have breakfast and doze on the way to market while her parents talked quietly beside her. In an extension, perhaps idealistic, of my enjoyment of the market, I have always thought that a girl brought up as she was, and the many like her, had a head start on being solid and resourceful and responsible adults, with an uncommon sense of balance.

But my main nostalgia is still for those Saturday mornings when my daughter was four or five and we would go to the market. She would stand on the car seat beside me; a dangerous practice I know, but she liked to see out. If I had to stop suddenly, I would throw one arm across to hold her in place. We talked and laughed and enjoyed the weekly ritual. Now we both have that to remember — I much older, on the downslope of the mountain, and she making her own chosen way, no longer a little girl whose eyes just barely cleared the counter at the place where the old lady, dead now, sliced little bits of her own sausage for us to taste and admire.

SCOTT YOUNG

Preface

IT ALL HAS TO COME FROM SOMEWHERE

ONE DAY, several yars ago now, Hans Zander was having supper with his friend Joso Spralja, a Toronto restaurant owner. Spralja (it seems odd to call him that, since most know him simply as Joso) was talking about his customers. Many of them, he said, kept asking where he got his fish, which was getting to be quite a nuisance. Didn't they know about the Newport Fish Market?

Obviously not. But Zander didn't know about it either — so he arranged to tag along one morning at the crack of dawn, when Joso went there to haggle with other seafood middlemen over the crates of fresh flounder, red snapper and squid. "It opened my eyes to the whole world of markets," Zander recalls. "Like most of us, I'd never really considered that all the things we eat have to come from somewhere, that they don't just materialize on our plates."

What Zander had discovered — what he set out to capture with sketchpad and paintbrush — was Ontario's living market tradition. In his travels, he found a complex network of commerce and culture, ranging from a single farmer's once-a-week stall to huge wholesale outlets, specialized auctions and almost-private, sometimes very powerful institutions. But all were markets under the skin — places were people would come to buy and sell.

He learned, for instance, that public markets — the kind you might visit on a Saturday morning — have staged a tremendous comeback these past few years. Every sizeable city is bound to have its market house — a building that springs to life at least one day a week, filled with the fruits and vegetables brought from nearby farming areas by market gardeners and small landowners whose kids stay home to man a roadside stand. But in the larger locations, you'll also find meat, fish, dairy products, fresh-baked breads and pastries, small livestock and homeless pets, local crafts and simply made music, perhaps a smattering of antiques and curious junk. A market has yet another definition: a place where people come to meet, to have a good time and to get in touch with one another. And that, in a somewhat depersonalized decade, seems a very healthy, very human, thing.

In Ontario alone there are more than eighty public markets, compared with a mere handful less than a generation ago. The same is true right across the country — Alberta went from four markets in the early 1970s to a hundred today. Nobody could have predicted this growth; it just seemed to happen of its own accord. In fact, in the 1950s, various "experts" were busily predicting the very opposite — that chain stores would wipe out the markets altogether. But many of us grew to distrust the big outlets, with their full-page newspaper ads and on-again, off-again bargains. We didn't want to lose contact with individual shopkeepers, so we kept on going to small street-corner stores. Ironically, the supermarkets responded by cutting back on overpackaging, letting us grope through, say, a binful of beans, instead of doling them out in preordained plastic bags. Too late! Because by that time, a lot of us had taken the next logical step, and were heading for a market to fill some portion of our weekly shopping basket.

We may not save a lot of money in the process, since many stalls are actually supplied by wholesalers, just like the chain stores. But that's not the point. The point is that we're dealing with a real live person on the other side of the counter, who's personally accountable for the goods he sells. If he's smart, he'll move heaven and earth to come up with the freshest, tastiest stock he can. If not, there's always the next booth — and he knows it. He may have other virtues, too. Chances are he isn't all that fond of metric, and knows a couple of half-decent jokes. Multiply that one person by a hundred, and you've got a market. And a market's most important ingredients — its flavour, colour, freedom of choice and sense of life — have no price tags.

But everything else *does*. That particular story changes very little with the passing years — and a look backwards in time to ancient Egypt, the *agora* of Athens or the *forum Romanum* (where, as always, the buyer had to beware) becomes a search for similarities, showing very clearly the beginnings of our modern-day trade and commerce.

The first markets were founded on barter — simple transactions between a farmer with food to spare but no plates to eat from and a tinsmith with precisely the opposite problem. But before long (to give the buyers a fighting chance, and to make life easier for sellers who moved from place to place), the markets began to generate systems of standardized weights and measures, widely recognized forms of money, and the first halting stabs at quality control. A stone carving, still visible above an Athens gateway, sets out regulations for the sale of olive oil. It dates from the second century — the early bite of what we'd call a government watchdog. But this kind of intervention was inevitable. The Greek and Roman marketplaces didn't exist in isolation. Rather, they were the focal points of city life, with law courts and fish stalls, Senates and religious shrines, all side by side. They grew and spread with their respective empires but lapsed into darkness when those empires fragmented and fell.

Throughout the feudal period, the whole concept of markets was put on hold, as fewer owners came to control more and more land. Tenant farmers were no better than slaves, surrendering their surplus crops to lords of the manor. But feudalism itself broke down, as newly prosperous cities emerged, complete with a newly prosperous middle class. And into the breach, up from dimly remembered ashes, came the medieval market and its blood relation, the fair.

In Britain — for better or worse, our line of descent — the right to establish a market was granted by royal charter to religious houses or local nobility. In return, they had to police the proceedings and punish merchants who "forestalled" by contracting business outside the market's boundaries, "engrossed" by inflating the cost of goods through hoarding and artificial shortages, or "regrated" by tacking on unjustified markups. (Today's consumer would surely feel right at home.) By the twentieth century, charter-holders had begun fortifying the marketplace (and so, by definition, the town itself) against roving bandits and enemies of the state. As a reward, they were allowed to collect a fee from the merchants and, in some cases, a toll from anyone entering the grounds. Many a cathedral's coffers overflowed — and many a new market town sprang up where none had been before.

By the fifteenth century, there were some eight hundred market towns in England and Wales. Each had its main intersection, where someone, usually the church, would erect a market hall, topped with its market cross (though this term soon came to mean the building itself). Once a central point was fixed, the town grew up around it, stretching up and down the high street in a straggling line of jerry-built structures called "shambles," followed by more permanent shops attached to craftsmen's houses. This growth spelled trouble for local officials, who'd previously had to wrestle with nothing more complex than the occasional "assize," which set the price of bread and ale. Now, however, they found it necessary to keep an eye on fast-buck "suburban" upstarts who persisted in opening their doors while the market was in operation. Shades of Sunday closing and the blue laws, alive and well in the fifteenth century! But on that note, let's leave these town fathers, knee-deep in a tangle of medieval red tape, and turn to the fortunes of the fair.

Fairs were granted by charter as well, to pretty much the same vested interests, but took place only once a year in the larger towns. They were linked to holidays or feast days, could last for weeks at a time, and seem to have been far racier (not to mention trickier) places than garden-variety markets. Some were held in local churchyards, which were soon awash in clowns and jugglers, fortune-tellers and merchants from the Continent peddling strange and wonderful goods. Before long, the churches began to lose their grip on the fairs, through both sheer numbers — 2,315 charters were granted between the years 1199 and 1483 — and an explosion of international trade. New sea routes brought even more exotic wares to the English countryside. Silks and spices came to shoulder out the local crafts, and a new breed of merchants appeared — men who would underwrite voyages overseas, offer a form of marine insurance, or lend money to a farmer against his next year's crop. Now, for the first time, people had to contend with the interest charges previously frowned on as usury. Deals were made on paper; interest-bearing notes were exchanged from fair to fair. Today's commodities brokers, bankers and speculators would have no difficulty recognizing the roots of their professions in these unsophisticated beginnings.

Our Canadian experience springs directly from this period of exploration and colonization. America's newly founded towns were keen to provide old world conveniences: New York had a weekly market in 1566, Boston in 1633. North of the border, we followed suit as quickly as possible. Windsor, Nova Scotia, hosted the continent's first agricultural fair in 1765, and holds it to this day. Queenston was the site of fairs by 1799; Kingston's market was established in 1801 and York's in 1804. By 1840 there were annual fairs in Guelph, Ottawa, Cobourg, Brantford and Hamilton — all of which, by this time, had their market as well. The most famous and persistent fair was the Toronto exhibition, what we know today as the CNE, founded in 1846. In fact, we seemed to like fairs so much that we kept on creating them well into the twentieth century. The Royal Agricultural Winter Fair kicked off in 1922, but it perpetuates a long-standing tradition of holding livestock sales in November, so that farmers can be rid of cattle they don't want to support through the long, hard winter months — a custom that might not occur to the modern-day city-dweller, who takes his seasons and his shows for granted.

Other "reasons why" have been lost as well, which seems a pity. Our traditions have become diverse, and scattered in time. But it all has to come from some-where, as Hans Zander's voyage of discovery made clear. The one-man stall — direct marketing at its most elemental and possibly its finest — is only the tip of an iceberg. Just as medieval moneychangers evolved into superspecialized financial wizards of the banking system, Zander's quest led from the humblest flea market to events as fine-tuned and (to most of us) otherworldly as the Woodbine Yearling Sale — an unsuspected galaxy of commercial activities, many of them caught under at least the partial thumb of government regulation. It's worth noting that Ontario is the only province that hasn't encouraged the spread of public markets by generous grants; they've made it entirely on their own, through visibility and accessibility. Not so the Ontario Flue-Cured Tobacco Manufacturers' (Marketing Board), which conducts auctions of pressing interest only to those who want to know exactly what's going into their cigarettes, and the Toronto Stock Exchange, whose high-voltage rituals seem light-years away from our monthly attempts to balance a simple chequebook.

We'll never have occasion to visit some of these places in the flesh — only by way of Zander's artistry. But that's okay. It's enough to know they're there, functioning much as they should, in all their diversity. There's a market for virtually everything civilization's been able to create — especially here in Ontario, where we're doubly fortunate to have such a wealth of products close to hand, as well as Canada's longest-established market buildings to house their sale.

As Zander learned, there's nothing alien about even the most obscure of them. His perceptive paintings and drawings show that he, like Scott Young, became a "market freak." Indeed, Zander's travels were in part a voyage of *re*discovery. Many of the sites he visited brought to mind memories of his childhood in a tiny village called Berka, in what is now East Germany, where gypsy caravans could be seen passing through the streets and life (until the east-west German border was established, running a stone's throw behind his family's backyard garden plot) was simpler, slower-paced and more direct. No wonder, then, that he should capture with such accuracy and zest the spirit of these seemingly dissimilar locations, working with an exacting combination of vibrant water-colours and India ink, as well as recording his first impressions in the reference sketches he often prefers to Polaroid photographs.

With this book, Hans Zander invites you to join him in becoming a convert to the marketplace — to which, in all its many forms, we bid you more than welcome.

A market has yet another definition: a place where people come to meet, to have a good time and to get in touch with one another. And that, in a somewhat depersonalized decade, seems a very healthy, a very human thing

The St. Lawrence Market, Toronto

Upstairs, the scene becomes even more chaotic. Here you gain a true sense of the building's size. Staring up 90 feet to the roofline, you think the place could be a barn once used as a cathedral, or maybe the other way around

The St. Lawrence Market

CHAUFFEURED CHEDDAR
AND THE GHOST OF JENNY LIND

AT TWO IN THE MORNING on a bone-chilling winter's Saturday, when farmers from as far as a hundred miles away start unloading their trucks in utter darkness, there are customers already hovering around the St. Lawrence Market. Some are shift workers, others just plain insomniacs, or perhaps chefs from certain downtown hotels, in search of both quality and quantity. Each one thinks he's sure to get the best selection, and has sacrificed his sleep to be first in line.

Then there are those who take the opposite tack — who delay their bargain-hunting until late afternoon, when the crowds have thinned and the sellers are eager to pack up and return to Streetsville, Alliston or the Holland Marsh. As for everybody else, the great mass of Torontonians comes between ten and two, just as city-dwellers have done for more than 175 years, with much the same expectations and to more or less the same spot.

In 1802, when Toronto was aptly known as Muddy York, they'd have had to settle for the tender mercies of William Cooper's Toronto Coffee House, a combination inn and general store that offered a choice of cash purchase or barter for "genteel board . . . viands [and] segars." Two years later, to everyone's relief, the first market was established by the lieutenant-governor, on the site of the present St. Lawrence Hall at King and Jarvis streets. The building was little more than a wooden shambles, and in 1831 it was razed to make way for an altogether more opulent brick structure, built around an open quadrangle with open arch-ways at the sides. A wooden gallery ran along the building's exterior, and in 1834 a portion collapsed during a political meeting. Several people were injured when they fell onto upturned hooks in the butcher shops below. The reason for this ill-timed gathering was that the market building also functioned as a town hall, and continued to do so even after the City of Toronto was incorporated that same year. (Ten years later, the councillors decided to build a new city hall at Jarvis and Front streets, where they continued to meet until the turn of the century. This structure became today's South Market.)

All these improvement schemes meant change enough, but by far the greatest turn in the market's fortunes came about by sheer chance. In 1849, a terrible fire swept through ten acres in the St. Lawrence ward, ending an era when the neighbourhood was *the* place to be seen, when proud citizens dressed to the nines and "did" King Street. The area south of King was devastated, and many merchants began rebuilding farther to the west, or north up Yonge Street. The market's facade was weakened by the flames, and collapsed. The building was demolished in 1850 to make way for the St. Lawrence Hall, completed later that same year and restored in 1967 as a Centennial project.

These new facilities provided both commercial space and a centre for all sorts of community activities. The third floor became Toronto's foremost concert hall; Jenny Lind sang there, and it isn't difficult, even now, to imagine her voice ringing through the auditorium. But despite these cultural breakthroughs, trade continued uninterrupted on the lower level, where lines of small shops on either side formed a 200-foot long arcade. Dry goods, drugs and books were sold here, mostly by shopkeepers who had larger premises uptown. At the back came innumerable butchers' stalls and "provisions dealers." Behind them, various out-buildings and additions crept south toward Front Street. This arrangement continued until 1901, when most trade shifted to the South Market, in the wake of departing civic politicians. The buildings behind the hall fell gradually into disrepair, and were torn down in 1968 to be replaced by the present North Market.

There's a distinct difference in the tone of the buildings as we view them today. The modern structure is coldly functional, built of brick and stark concrete, but it comes alive when occupied. Strangely enough, this is where the *real* farmers come to rent their Saturday spaces, for as little as five dollars a table. Fresh sausages pile up unwrapped and in the open; bushel baskets of unwashed vegetables overflow onto the sidewalk. A free-and-easy approach to packaging seems

the rule; prices are scrawled with crayon on folded-over paper bags hung from strings. Many shoppers seem to believe that this building, with its total lack of sophistication, offers better value for money. One Saturday morning, not too long before his death, Lord Thomson of Fleet was spotted in the North Market, making a purchase. He carefully chose a wheel of cheese, then summoned his chauffeur, who gravely handed him a wallet. Thomson extracted the correct change, handed both wallet and cheese back to the chauffeur, and departed with a grace befitting one of Canada's wealthiest men — the master and his Cheddar, whisked away in a huge brown limousine.

The restored South Market, on the other hand, is open Tuesday through Saturday, and has a somewhat more trendy atmosphere. The building is cavern-ously huge, and takes forever to get through on a crowded weekend. In the basement are an amazing variety of stalls, in addition to those selling basic meats and vegetables. Fishmongers are out in force, along with men who sell 89-cent pantyhose, helium-filled balloons and mildly naughty novelties. Like vendors everywhere, they like to heighten the drama by calling out their wares in the loudest possible voices. Journalist Harry Bruce once captured their style to per-fection. "Some of the guys who yell at you down there," he wrote, "try to make pigs' feet sound like a strip show, and a bag of tripe like a bingo game."

Upstairs, the scene becomes even more chaotic. Here you gain a true sense of the building's size; staring up ninety feet to the roofline, you think the place could be a barn once used as a cathedral, or maybe the other way around. The ceiling traps the hubbub, bouncing it back as a constant, unvarying din. Flower vendors tout their wares amid lush splashes of colour, and everywhere you look are bewildering arrays of food: thirty kinds of tea, two dozen blends of coffee, jugs of apple cider, jars of spiced olives, dill, watercress and parsley in long white plastic tubes, couscous, popping corn by the bushel, toasted buckwheat, thirty-pound containers of onions and something or other (maybe even pecans) in old gunny sacks stencilled "Basher Pecan Company, Valdosta, Georgia, USA." Add to this the strolling musicians both classical and folk, small children who've momentarily mislaid their parents and a pack of lottery ticket salesmen screaming out the chances of instant fortune and you've got an atmosphere that makes the medieval fairground seem tranquil and tame.

It would take a bit of time, and some very shrewd comparison shopping, but it seems that prices in the South Market are a bit higher than those across Front Street. But so is the overhead. Vendors may soon be paying up to $19 per square foot — about the same as renting downtown office space. But slightly more expensive goods are the price of continuity. Some of the market's stalls — the ones with old iron grills that pull down and lock at closing time — have been in the same family for two or three generations. It's not uncommon to see mother and daughter, grandfather and grandson, working side by side in white aprons, serving up the mounds of beefsteak tomatoes or trays of Queen's Plate Special Extra Lean Mince. These vendors are the market's permanent fixtures — more so than the ersatz antiques that decorate a nearby restaurant's walls. Their faces are known to hundreds, maybe thousands of truly satisfied customers — people who never learned their names, but keep returning year after year for the quality of their goods and the warmth of a welcoming smile. And even though today's vendors deal strictly in cash on the barrelhead, the market hasn't seen the last of barter. When Hans Zander went there with his Polaroid camera, a fishmonger offered him a fresh trout in exchange for an instant souvenir, and Zander instantly made the trade.

The Kensington Market, Toronto

If you plan to haggle over the price, it helps to speak the right language. This usually isn't English, but one of Kensington's pleasures, along with the bargain-hunting imperative, is seeing how well everybody gets along

The Kensington Market

HALF THE WORLD IN A DOZEN CITY BLOCKS

IF the St. Lawrence Market gets points for continuity, then the Kensington Market ought to be cherished for its complete and utter absence. Kensington is something completely different, something uniquely Canadian and very much Toronto. It wasn't established by decree — it simply grew, literally out of control from the very first. And from the first, it has constantly changed as one immigrant group replaced or joined the others.

Kensington is an ethnic market, packed into a cramped and noisy quarter to the southwest of College Street and Spadina Avenue. Its merchants are mainly Portuguese, Chinese, Jewish, Latin American and West Indian — though today's breakdown may be outmoded next month or year. Certainly the ratio of any one group to the others is in constant flux; and the market's activity, which goes on year round, six days a week and as many as sixteen hours a day, isn't confined to a single market building. In fact, the maze of houses and shops that make up Kensington Market was never meant to be a market at all.

In the 1870s, an area to the west of Spadina was opened to developers, who rose to the challenge with block upon block of the latest model row housing, and proudly named the streets: Augusta, Nassau, Oxford and Wales. But at the turn of the century, when the original residents were moving up in the world, and out to new suburban hinterlands north of Bloor Street, Kensington was flooded with Polish and Russian Jews. In 1901, a tiny street called Kensington Place was 80 percent Anglo. Ten years later, it had become 100 percent Jewish.

Naturally, the new arrivals set up kosher shops, which attracted Jews from other parts of the city. Pushcarts filled the narrow streets, and dry goods businesses began to spread south down Spadina. A synagogue was established nearby in 1912, the market itself was firmly entrenched by 1914, and by 1920 Kensington was the centre of Jewish commercial life. Until the 1940s, the market's shops were confined to one or two larger streets with the smaller byways given over to pedlars and pushcart owners. But immediately after the Second World

War, the Jews were joined by great numbers of other European immigrants, starting Kensington on both an overnight expansion program and its incredibly patchwork path.

A strong Jewish presence remains today, though the Poles and Ukrainians who followed them have pulled up stakes, moving west along Bloor Street to Roncesvalles. After the war came Italians and Greeks, but they too tended to disperse. In the 1960s and 1970s, however, there was a downright invasion of Portuguese, who've hung in to dominate the area. But more recent entrants include South Americans, West Indians and the longer-established Chinese, who started moving up Spadina from Dundas when the downtown building boom first threatened Old Chinatown to the south.

Given these somewhat hectic circumstances, you'd expect the most numerous group would squeeze the others out, virtually driving them elsewhere. That's what happened in several of Toronto's strictly residential areas. At the very least, you'd think the market would fragment, breaking down into ethnic mini-sections along clearly defined lines. But one of Kensington's great joys is that no such thing has come to pass. It's true that the Chinese influence is concentrated at the market's southern boundaries, with the Portuguese most visible to the north around Oxford and Nassau streets, and the South Americans gaining ground between Baldwin and St. Andrew's. But in fact, the various groups seem thoroughly mixed, like a well-shuffled deck of cards, with a surprising amount of cross-pollination and adaptation. Many old Jewish stores, like the Imperial Poultry & Egg Market on Baldwin Street, are no longer kosher — and just down the street, the Royal Food Centre (a Jewish shop still run by its founding family) is doing good trade in goat meat and other Caribbean delicacies. That's why the only safe prediction is that today's Portuguese emporium may soon be catering to the tastebuds of some other group we can only dimly imagine.

Most of Kensington's buildings were originally single-family homes, and for years the city gnashed its teeth at the sight of ground floors converted into retail stores, tiny yards pressed into service as a showcase for a merchant's goods. In time, the civic authorities did the only sensible thing. They threw up their hands, and let Kensington run its own erratic course. This lack of control over a space that was cramped to begin with lends urgency to an atmosphere in which you can buy (or stumble over) the following, noted during the course of Hans Zander's visit: fresh octopuses, imported reggae LPs, freshly skinned rabbits, vinyl overcoats, pigeon eggs, newly plucked geese, exotic cheeses, religious pictures, rainbow trout and smelt. And if the streets get *too* overbearing, there's refuge of sorts in the cafés, poolrooms and shops that serve as meeting places for the cultural salad, their entranceways plastered with business cards in a dozen

different tongues, advertising driving schools, insurance agencies, and painting, decorating or babysitting services.

Back on the streets, if you plan to haggle over the price, it helps to speak the right language. This usually isn't English, but one of Kensington's pleasures, along with the bargain-hunting imperative, is seeing how well everybody gets along, in spite of the odd cultural collision. As historian Robert Harney has pointed out, in Kensington there's "a special effort to understand one another.

The small moments of conflict are noticed for that reason. The Portuguese fishmonger asks an elderly Chinese lady not to squeeze each blue crab before buying, and she goes away insulted. A suburban school child, 'gawking at the immigrants' along with her class, asks a Jewish woman to pose in front of her poultry store; the woman, speaking to no one in particular, remarks that she is as Canadian as the visitors and has lost a son in the Canadian Armed Forces. A Metropolitan Toronto policeman gives out parking tickets as if he were a French or British soldier defending the city from Indians."

That's the kind of atmosphere the Canadian Broadcasting Corporation's television series *King of Kensington* merely hinted at, without ever capturing or re-creating — perhaps because, at the risk of sounding like a bad speech by the deputy minister of immigration, Kensington isn't just a slice of life, but a ragged, unmanageable hunk of *real* life in the raw. When anything threatens the common interest of the market community, everyone turns out to help. If a skinny white chicken escapes from its wooden cage and makes a mad dash for freedom somewhere east of Spadina, a dozen merchants and passersby join its owner in an attempt to recapture it, hurling curses at the hapless bird in umpteen different languages, a Keystone Kops routine in desperate need of subtitles. Soon the entire neighbourhood seems to be running, tripping in long aprons, clutching bags of groceries. Just as everyone starts laughing, the owner finally catches up with his prey, and does what seems appropriate in the circumstances. He is, after all, a butcher, with a job of work to do. He kills the chicken by chopping off its head. The laughter stops, and everybody goes about his business.

The Byward Market, Ottawa

Of all the markets he visited, Hans Zander found Byward's the most attractively laid-out, with one stand more beautiful than the next

The Byward Market

COMPETITIVE CARNATIONS AND
CLIENTS FROM EMBASSY ROW

OTTAWA'S BYWARD MARKET has a character all its own, for several reasons. First, it's located in the heart of the nation's capital, and caters to the members of various diplomatic corps, adding multicultural flavour to an already bicultural scene. Also, of all the markets he visited, Hans Zander found Byward the most attractively laid out. "One stand was more beautiful than the next," he recalls. "There seemed to be a healthy competition going on between the vendors over who could have the very best display."

Ottawa's first market was established in Lower Town in 1846, when Ottawa was still the village of Bytown, named in honour of Colonel John By, who laid out the street plan in 1826 while his Royal Engineers were constructing the Rideau Canal. There was no market building at first — only an open area on George Street, where farmers sold their goods from carts and hastily improvised stands. It was successful from the first, and should have deterred potential rivals, but the town was growing fast — incorporated as a town in 1850, renamed the city of Ottawa five years later, and made the capital of the United Province of Canada.

This rapid growth had prompted a leading businessman named Nicholas Sparks to conceive the idea of starting a second market on Elgin Street, the site of the present-day National Arts Centre. Sparks donated this land to the city, hoping that a "West Ward Market" would increase the value of surrounding properties, which he conveniently happened to own. A large building with a sharply peaked roof and a bell tower was duly erected, but the buying public responded by staying away in droves, so the ever-resourceful Sparks was reduced to inviting city council to use the upper storey as its chambers.

While Sparks was up to these and other tricks, a notorious event quite literally rocked the Byward Market. In 1849, political tempers were running high over the Rebellion Losses Bill, which indemnified everyone except convicted traitors for damage done to property during the uprisings of 1837-38. This pleased Reformers, but outraged the Tories, some of whom displayed their pique by burning down the parliament buildings in Montreal.

In any case, the Bill had been approved by Lord Elgin, the governor general, and news that he was planning an official visit to Bytown caused considerable stir. Arguments arose over the manner of his reception. A meeting was called at the Byward Market to discuss the issue, but the evening ended in a wild mêlée when the speaker's platform collapsed. People brandished guns and spilled outside onto the street, where snipers in nearby buildings took potshots and threw bricks at the crowd below. One man was killed and many injured, troops were called in to calm things down, and the date entered local history as Stony Monday.

When Sparks's building (which had in fact been serving as council chambers) was abandoned in 1877, the Byward Market — the one that worked all along — looked remarkably as it does today, judging by photographs of the period. But as the twentieth century wore on, the market and its immediate neighbourhood ran down. Then, about ten years ago, the building was given a thorough renovation, along with several structures on the west side of the square, including the Lapointe fish store on Dalhousie Street, one of the oldest commercial properties in the city.

A happy result of the revamping was a permanent crafts market inside the market house, complementing the Byward tradition of selling produce out-of-doors, from two hundred and fifty stalls. In addition to the usual meats, breads and vegetables, Zander found one or two specialists in mangoes, plantains and kiwi fruit, as well as several dealers in sod. Influenced perhaps by tales of free-spending mandarins, he expected the Byward's customers to show up in civil service suits or arrive, Lord-Thomson-like, in limousines — and was mildly disappointed when the only touch of pomp and circumstance turned out to be a marching band that played inspiring tunes as he sketched.

The Hamilton Farmers' Market

So while the city has become a thriving industrial centre, its market remains an urban oasis, a symbol of rich agricultural lands beyond the smokestacks

The Hamilton Farmers' Market

AN UNSUSPECTED SIDE OF ONTARIO'S STEELTOWN

IN 1833, when Hamilton's population numbered some two thousand souls, its citizens gathered to consider three major expenditures. They wanted to simultaneously provide a headquarters for a "board of police" (which functioned as the local government), purchase a fire engine and erect a public market. The pumper seems to have taken priority, but a market of sorts did in fact spring up, in somewhat cramped quarters on John Street. It had, at first, space for a mere eight stalls. Perhaps this is why the legislators disdained it as a meeting place, preferring to gather at the brand new firehall or in a nearby tavern.

In any case, a rival market reared its head in 1837, on far more central James Street. Two years later when its building was completed, city council (having replaced the police board in 1846) was quick to move in, remaining until 1889. The John Street site fell into disrepair, lingering on as an outlet for hay and firewood. It's long since demolished, though its former location remains known as Haymarket Square.

The James Street market, however, remained intact, and you can visit it today, downstairs from a branch of the public library. When Hans Zander arrived at seven one Saturday morning, the place was so packed he couldn't find a spot to sit and sketch. Sunlight flooded in through huge windows, illuminating hand-painted signs that proudly read "Meadowgreen Farms," "Garden Lane" and "From the Valley." So while Hamilton has become a thriving industrial centre, its market remains an urban oasis, a symbol of rich agricultural lands beyond the smokestacks, and a convenient outlet for produce from the Niagara fruit belt to the south.

The Windsor City Market

Essex County's mild climate and longer growing season mean that the market is often first out with peaches, melons, onions, tomatoes, peas and corn

The Windsor City Market

REBIRTH ALONG THE BORDER

WHEN WINDSOR'S MARKET was first established in 1858, it shared a building with the town hall. Twenty-one years later, this arrangement had proved unworkable, because the market — not the city government — had grown too large. So the market moved from Sandwich Street to its present location between Market and Chatham streets, on the eastern fringe of the downtown business district.

Today's vendors include farmers from Essex, Kent and Lambton counties and dealers supplied by wholesale firms. All of them operate six days a week, from a masonry building covering about half a city block. (Its construction in 1929 was something of an act of faith, for by then the market had dwindled to a shed, the scene of dog shows and wrestling matches.) But the venture paid off, and today's two hundred and fifty active stalls attract knowledgeable buyers who come from far afield in search of freshness and variety. There may be little difference in price between the stalls and local supermarkets — but the market remains the best place to take advantage of the region's mild climate and longer growing season, which means that Essex is often first out with peaches, melons, onions, tomatoes, peas and corn. Homemade specialties are available as well; Hans Zander found several stands dispensing spicy sausages, brought by livestock owners who butcher their own pigs, curing the meat in an old-fashioned way. And, of all the sites he visited, Zander found that Windsor's market offers the most dramatic view, across the river to the Detroit skyline.

The Waterloo Farmers' Market
and Stockyards

Moving in from Kitchener as if it were the most natural thing in all the world, the Mennonites began to sell their goods from stalls inside and from truck beds or makeshift tables in the surrounding lot

thirty miles southeast — but a public market existed somewhere in Kitchener-Waterloo by 1839, and more were definitely held in and around the town hall during the 1860s. These were make-do quarters at best, but it wasn't until 1907 that a building was erected specifically to house the market.

Here was a market to be reckoned with — an imposing structure with four hundred stalls on two storeys, aisle upon aisle of ever more delicious food. In time, the Kitchener Farmers' Market came to be known as the finest of its kind, and a major tourist attraction. On a Saturday morning as many as thirty thousand people would arrive, including literal busloads from Toronto and New York State. They came in spring for dandelion greens, in autumn for fruits and in wintertime for ducks, geese and free-range turkeys. They came year round for sausage and sauerkraut and sinfully rich desserts, pork hocks and pies, chocolates and cheeses. It was, while it lasted, a stationary feast.

For many visitors, the Mennonites were an attraction in themselves. In his introduction to *A Splendid Harvest*, J. Russell Harper recalls his boyhood impressions of the market during the 1920s:

The real fascination for me was in mixing with the local German farm people who stood waiting for customers. Mennonite women were dressed in conservative garb of sombre grays and blacks as they placidly tended their stalls. About them was such a quiet shyness that it seemed immodestly rude to stare at their dress and faces. But when one dared to steal a glance, it was possible to read there a combination of gentle ways complemented by great strength of character; this firmness was echoed in the solidity of their menfolk. They were a people to be remembered.

Harper also writes that the Mennonites' "toughness of moral and physical fibre" was "delicately balanced by the contentment in the melodious touches and sparkling accents of colour" in their crafts. A quilt, an apron or a prayer cap bought in those early days would be a prized possession indeed, the centrepiece of an expensive collection.

All these elements magically combined to produce an atmosphere unlike that of any other market. But magic seldom lasts — and in 1971, the city of Kitchener announced a plan that would change the market's fate forever.

Basically, the scheme involved razing both market and city hall, and selling the vacant land, along with another site across the street, to a developer, who would construct in their place a parking garage to accommodate seven hundred and fifty cars, a shopping mall, a department store and a twelve-storey office building with five floors leased back to the city fathers. Plans were laid in a secretive manner, and the story only became public knowledge thanks to a student newspaper, rather than any of the established local media — prompting anti-development groups to charge a conspiracy of silence.

Controversy raged throughout the year, and drew a surprising amount of national attention. Clearly, the Kitchener situation touched a nerve in other cities, where urban activists were fighting to preserve all sorts of neighbourhoods. But in December, the citizens of Kitchener voted overwhelmingly to proceed with the redevelopment, and the old market was demolished in August, 1973.

There's still a Kitchener market today — four hundred and thirty stalls that continue to draw the tourists each weekend. But most of the Mennonites have gone — made uncomfortable by the glossy surroundings, resentful perhaps of intrusion or betrayal by the state. Slowly but surely they withdrew to other, smaller markets — reviving and changing them just as they did in Kitchener's golden age.

Hans Zander didn't know all this had taken place. So, after a false start in Kitchener, he made his way to the Waterloo Farmers' Market, on Weber Street, in the northern outskirts of Waterloo, where he found all the Mennonites he could wish for. A building had stood there since 1910, but had fallen on hard times and bingo games, and was replaced in 1966 — just in time for the Mennonites to make it their own. Moving in from Kitchener as if it were the most natural thing in all the world, they began to sell their goods from stalls inside, from truck beds and makeshift tables in the surrounding lot. Zander knew he was on the right track when he saw their buggies heading for town along the highway, and their horses stabled in a nearby shed.

But when he tried to take reference photographs of the Mennonite vendors to supplement his sketches, they seemed to shy away. A bystander was quick to explain: the Old Order considers the camera to be sinful, because it presents things exactly as they appear, contrary to an Old Testament commandment ("Thou shalt not make unto thee any graven image or any likeness of anything that is in heaven above, or that is in the earth beneath, or that is in the waters under the earth.") Fortunately, Zander managed to explain his motives in fluent German, earning a sort of wary acceptance. The Mennonites concluded that if he insisted in idolatry it would be his mistake, not theirs.

Once he'd overcome that particular barrier, Zander went on to appreciate the market's quality. Almost all the goods were homemade, home-grown or home-sewn. There were wooden toys and knitted sweaters, soaps and summer sausages, eggs, honey and cheeses from surrounding farms.

THE KITCHENER-WATERLOO STOCKYARDS

Zander came back the following week, and went to the Kitchener-Waterloo Stockyards, which he found immense and somewhat intimidating. Hundreds of trucks arrive here every Thursday, and trading lasts all day, with separate auction rings for beef cattle and calves, pigs, rabbits and chickens. Caught amid the incredible noise produced by several hundred unwilling cows, Zander was re-minded of the stories he'd read as a boy about the great Chicago slaughterhouses — and decided that an open-air market was perhaps a more congenial and certainly more peaceful location.

The Elmira Maple Syrup Festival

Hans Zander arrived one rather wintry April day, but found the main street so jammed with visitors he didn't know where to begin. So he decided instead to go to the source of it all — a tiny sugar shack, set in the bushland to the west of town

The Elmira Maple Syrup Festival

SOWS, SAP BUCKETS AND SUGAR SHACKS

I N THE LATE 1850s, Elmira's original settlers were joined by an influx of new arrivals with names like Ruppel, Wehners, Reising and Weitzel. Many of these German immigrants began raising hogs — and, about 1865, they launched the Elmira Pig Fair.

Until the Grand Trunk Railway arrived in 1891, followed by the Canadian Pacific in 1906, Elmira had no rail connection to Ontario's larger centres. Farmers had to butcher their stock and bring it into town, where a middleman carted it the twenty miles southeast to Guelph. But with the coming of the railway, pigs and other animals could be transported live, producing a massive increase in volume. In a typical year, Elmira shipped twelve thousand hogs, a thousand sheep, over five thousand cattle and several hundred horses — not bad for a community that numbered at most a few hundred people, and wasn't incorporated as a town until 1923.

By this time, Pig Day ("the first Monday before the second Tuesday of each month, rain or shine") had become a major event, where farmers gathered to exchange all manner of livestock. Many of the participants were Mennonites, who'd gained vast experience with heavy draught horses in the United States.

The old pig fair waxed and waned throughout the twentieth century, ending in the 1960s. But in April of 1965, enterprising citizens began the Elmira Maple Syrup Festival, which was an immediate success. Then, in 1972, came the weekly event called *Der Bauer Mark* (or farmers' market) — filled with year-round maple sugar vendors, as well as local craftspeople with handmade dolls and hooked rugs to sell.

A SUGAR SHACK WEST OF ELMIRA

Following the demolition of the old Kitchener market, and the subsequent dispersal of the Mennonites, Elmira began to attract even larger crowds. Hans Zander drove down one rather wintry April day, hoping to catch the festivities in full swing, but found the main street so jammed with visitors he didn't know where to begin. So he decided instead to go to the source of it all — and found what he wanted in a tiny sugar shack, set in the bushland ten miles west of town.

The Stouffville Sales Barn

Tables and stalls occupy every corner of the huge structure, and buyers can expect to find everything from cabbages to carpet remnants, licence plates to livestock, mismatched dishes to baby ducks

The Stouffville Sales Barn

DUNKERS, DOUGHNUTS AND
THE NON-NEGOTIABLE RABBIT

THE MARKET at Stouffville, some thirty miles northeast of Toronto, is a favourite of many people in search of a genuine country market within easy driving distance. Through the years, the area has remained an excellent source of honey and apple cider — "luxury" items which for decades would supplement the meagre incomes of local farmers. But it's no longer a centre for the Mennonites, their produce and handicrafts. In fact, it's easy to forget that Mennonites were Stouffville's founders.

In 1802, two Pennsylvania Mennonites, Peter Reesor and his brother-in-law Abraham Stouffer, came north to Upper Canada, investigating the possibility of resettlement in Markham and Whitchurch townships. Within a dozen years there were nearly sixty other families, including the Focklers, Groffs, Herrs, Hubers, Kreiders and Nichwanders. Most were Mennonites, but some were German Lutherans or Dunkers (an offshoot of the German Baptists).

Little is known about their market practices until the early twentieth century, when a weekly gathering was held on Civic Street, in what later became the town's municipal offices. This was distinct from a second "Dutch Market," located in the now demolished Daley Hall, where farmers rented stalls for five cents a day, a dollar per year. It took place on the first Thursday of every month and, according to one local historian, this became a "calendar day, a Dutch Picnic" — indicating that the monthly event was as much a social and cultural happening as a purely financial concern.

Today, farmers bring their produce to the Stouffville Sales Barn and Stock-yards, located on Highway 47 just to the north of town. This is also the home of the Big Flea Market — no exaggeration, as Hans Zander learned. He'd never seen so many different items under one roof. Tables and stalls occupy every corner of the huge structure, and buyers can expect to find everything from cabbages to carpet remnants, licence plates to livestock, mismatched dishes to baby ducks. And if you can't find what you're looking for inside, there are still more tables out-of-doors.

While a friend of Zander's was haggling over a stuffed alligator (for reasons known only to herself), the artist was offered a lonesome rabbit in return for one of his sketches. This time Zander declined. He already had a rabbit back at home — bought for two dollars, two weeks earlier in the Kensington Market.

The Newport Fish Market, Toronto

Rows of wildly dissimilar fish, oceans apart in nature, are manhandled into position side by side: blue runners and silver mullet, octopuses and horse mackerel, baby clams and conger eels the size of telephone poles

The Newport Fish Market

HIGH BIDS, BULK SQUIDS AND MARTY FELDMAN EYES

THE NEWPORT FISH MARKET, located at Dufferin and Dupont streets in Toronto's predominantly Italian west end, supplies retail fish shops and seafood restaurants with every conceivable variety of fresh- and salt-water creature, from the tiniest minnows to hundred-pound leviathans. It opened in 1965, the brainchild of a Portuguese-Canadian named Tercio Dias, at a time when local dining places were only just emerging from a culinary bog. Canned peas and overcooked beef were the orders of a given day, and adventurous eating consisted of a foray to darkest Chinatown for sweet and sour pork. In all, a sad affair — and a risky atmosphere in which to launch a business based on the idea that people would pay a premium for freshness and selection. But Dias took his chances, hoping to wean the more adventurous restaurateurs away from their former, largely American, sources.

One of the facts of Canadian Maritime life is that it's cheaper to send a fully-loaded truckful of fish to America's eastern seaboard than to dispatch a half-empty trailer from Halifax to Toronto. That's why an American connection remains. Crabs from Chesapeake Bay are trucked live via New York to Toronto, where frisky specimens command the going rate, while their slow-moving brethren sell at a discount, like wilted vegetables. Even the catch from our Maritime fisheries — the summer squid, perch, flounder, halibut, mackerel and herring — is sold back to Canadians after passing through the States. For most of his stock, Dias looks to the East Coast: Boston for sea trout and monkey fish, Florida for its grouper, kingfish, B-liner, red snapper and baby sharks, and Long Island Sound for oysters, clams, mussels, porgy and whiting.

Most of these are picked up from American terminals by forty-foot refrigerated trucks, and driven nonstop to the Toronto site. Fish from Portugal, Greece and other European countries are flown (packed in ice but never frozen) into Toronto International Airport, where they're met by Dias's men.

The Newport is a strange and somewhat eerie sight, especially as things begin at five in the morning, six days a week. Dias's employees are mainly Portuguese-Canadian, but his customers comprise a mini United Nations. It's not unusual to hear Greeks, Italians, East Indians, Chinese, Japanese and Yugoslavs all shouting simultaneously, somehow communicating with one another as they watch the workers unload a fleet of trucks packed with hundreds of boxes, baskets and sacks. Each container has been packed with countless tiny ice cubes, the kind you see in cocktail bars, which rattle around the crowded floor. Everyone wears special gloves with palms like sandpaper, to keep a grip on the increasingly slippery goods; everyone receives a long steel hook to rip open the wooden crates and drag purchases to some corner of the room for a final tally. Rows of wildly dissimilar fish — oceans apart in nature — are manhandled into position side by side. The buyers know them at a glance, and can spot kingfish, muttonfish, blue runners and silver mullet the instant a crate appears. But some species are so appallingly distinctive that even an amateur could tell them apart: conger eels the size of telephone poles, octopuses and scabbard fish, horse mackerel and baby clams.

These exotic specimens add much to Newport's atmosphere, but most clients prefer old standbys. These are often in short supply, and tempers flare when the day's trucks disgorge a mere half-dozen cases of red snapper. That's why many buyers stay up all night long, grimly determined to be first in line. But choice is only one reason for prompt attendance. A ten-inch snapper requires just as much time and effort to prepare as a two-hundred-pound Warsaw, so a shrewd chef will seek the middle ground. He'll also check each fish for freshness — first by peering into its eyes. (Epicure, the anonymous food critic of *Toronto Life* magazine, recommends a bulging gaze "something like Marty Feldman's.") Then, if still in doubt, he'll look for discolouration in the gills — and as a last resort, he'll give the thing a fast and conclusive sniff.

The Tillsonburg Tobacco Auction

As the numbered bundles are sent to the viewing area, they run a gauntlet of specialized employees: string-cutters, code-men, bale-tossers, scalemen, ticket-caretakers, dispatchers and whitecoat men — each with his precise function to perform in an unexpectedly formidable bureaucracy

The Tillsonburg Tobacco Auction

LEAF, CUTTERS AND LUGS, GRADED SIX WAYS FROM SUNDOWN

FOREIGNERS have a hard time believing that Canada's climate can produce good tobacco at all. Even many Canadians, especially in the frigid West, find the notion a bit much to swallow. But in fact, we're the world's fifth-largest tobacco grower (after China, the United States, Brazil and India). The annual crop, at $381 million, comes a respectable sixth in the nation's agricultural economy.

Granted, tobacco-growing areas are few and far between. Only seven percent of the crop comes from Quebec and the Maritime provinces. The vast majority ($362 million-worth in 1981) is grown in and around Ontario's Norfolk County, along the northern shore of Lake Erie between Windsor on the west and the Niagara Peninsula on the east. Here, in the towns of Delhi, Tillsonburg and Aylmer — all within twenty-five miles of one another — the tobacco is sold to cigarette manufacturers and international brokers from forty countries.

There's never been one central market for tobacco, and even the present system is relatively recent, even though the crop had flourished in this same area for hundreds of years before the arrival of European settlers. (The Petun tribe who once occupied the region are sometimes called the Tobacco Indians, and used it in their ceremonies; but early colonizers took no interest in its cultivation.)

Close to Lake Erie, the land is light and sandy. For generations, farmers did little better than squeak by at a subsistence level. But in 1919, two local men had the presence of mind to send a batch of soil samples to an Ottawa agricultural laboratory, asking what in heaven's name could thrive under such conditions. The lab, to its credit, suggested tobacco, and from then on the crop became a mainstay of the area.

Selling the stuff was another story altogether. In early years, cigarette companies simply engaged in "barn buying" — going from farm to farm paying cash on delivery, as they still do in Atlantic Canada. But during the Depression, when crops declined and other countries enacted tariffs to keep out foreign products, the tobacco growers decided to organize — to set up a self-help association.

What emerged, after a couple of false starts, was the Flue-Cured Tobacco Marketing Association of Ontario (now the Ontario Flue-Cured Tobacco Marketing Board), regulated by an act of the provincial legislature. It's a bewildering organization to the uninitiated, and trying to fathom how deals are made at the three auction exchanges (as the market houses are officially known) can be a perplexing business.

The process starts on the district's three thousand farms. In September, after the crops are harvested, the tobacco is gathered into "sticks" or bundles, then "flue-cured" by processing in drying kilns.

Now the confusion begins in earnest. When the markets open that month, the farmers have already done some preliminary grading. The system is based on colour: bright, dark, light green, dark green, red and ND (for "nondescript"). Next come independent graders working for both farmer and buyer, who mentally break each plant into three sections, calling the topmost leaves the "leaf" or B tobacco, the middle leaves the "cutters" or C tobacco, and the lower ones the "lugs" or X tobacco. Each of the three categories in turn is divided into seven colour variants: L for lemon-coloured, or F (we told you it gets confusing) for light mahogany. And if this weren't enough, they then break *those* divisions into six quality factors, running from Six for poor to One for choice.

Now they can label what they inspect with an extremely high degree of accuracy. For example, they might mark a bundle BL1, or lemon-coloured leaf of choice quality. But things don't stop there. The categories and sub-categories seem to go on forever. Weird as it sounds, there are five different grades of "nondescript," which is surely a contradiction in terms. In addition, ten special factors are expressed as final letters. An "H", for example, signifies hail damage — so BL6H means lemon-coloured leaf of poor quaity that's been worked over by the elements.

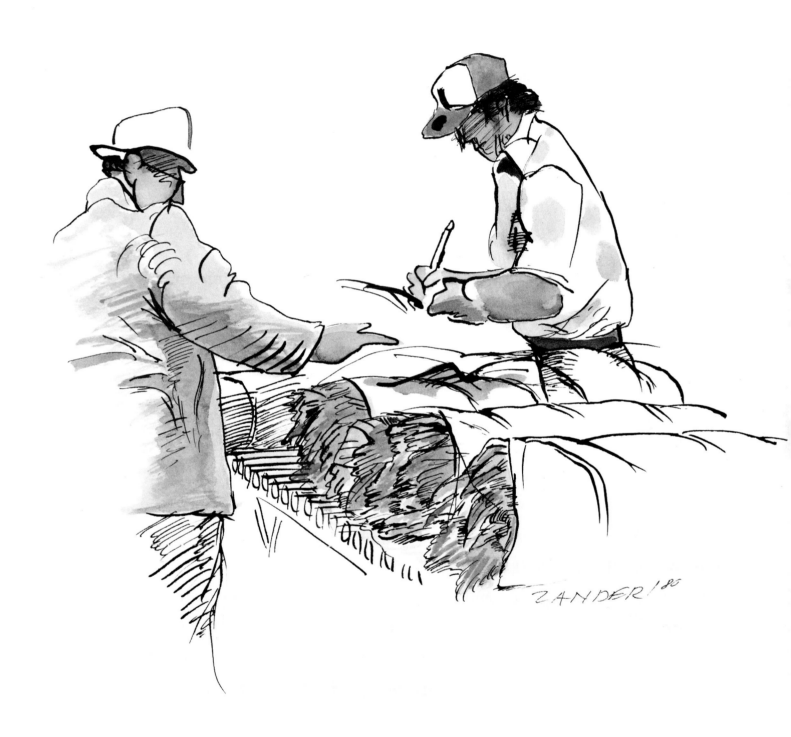

The auctions themselves are in some ways just as strange and drawn-out. Farmers bring in their pre-graded lots at predetermined times, to ensure the greatest possible variety on the bidding floor. As numbered bundles are sent along to the viewing area, they run a gauntlet of specialized marketing board employees. There are string-cutters, code-men, bale-tossers, scalemen, ticket-caretakers, dispatchers and whitecoat men (people in lab smocks who might be compared to floor walkers in department stores) — each with his precise function to perform, in an unexpectedly formidable bureaucracy.

Another odd feature of tobacco sales is that the bidding takes place in reverse. This is known as a Dutch Auction. The auctioneers start with the highest plausible figure, and work downward instead of up; the bidder makes his offer when the figure drops to a price he's prepared to pay. Bids are registered on an overhead electronic board called the Dutch Clock, which looks vaguely like a prop from one of the more frantic television quiz shows. But all this hocus-pocus is in fact necessary, because tobacco buyers are *very* particular. Each brand of cigarette is a combination of as many as twenty different tobacco grades, and one company can produce a dozen or more individual brands.

Like all marketing boards, the tobacco growers' association was designed to level out the dramatic swings in price between good years and bad. And it's been remarkably successful — during the 1970s, Ontario crops fluctuated between $1.25 and $1.35 a pound. Perhaps Hans Zander was sensitive to this feeling of tight control, when he hesitantly inquired whether he might smoke on the premises. He needn't have worried. "Please," the manager replied. "That's exactly what we *want* you to do."

The Ontario Food Terminal, Toronto

Hans Zander sat in the huge parking lot, waiting for enough light to sketch by, and counted the vans belonging to his neighbourhood grocery stores. They reminded him of the brightly painted gypsy wagons that passed through his childhood village

The Woodbine Yearling Sale, Toronto

For most people who aren't born into the world of racing, the sale's real interest lies not in the horses, most of which are reserved, dignified and quite beautiful, but in the bidders, who project entirely opposite qualities

The Woodbine Yearling Sale

Hip numbers and high rollers

ONE OF THE province's most exclusive and specialized auctions is the Woodbine Yearling Sale, held shortly after Labour Day by the Canadian Thoroughbred Horse Society. Every year, Ontario breeders register some eight hundred colts and fillies. Of these, about half are kept by their owners, and will probably be raced when they're two years old. (To simplify the arithmetic, all thoroughbreds are considered to have been born on January 1 — joining British monarchs in the distinction of an official as well as an actual birthday.) But the remainder are sold, to stable owners, trainers, entrepreneurs, the odd social climber and — especially in recent years — syndicates of less-than-very-wealthy folk, who spread the risk by pooling purchase costs.

The site is the Woodbine track, in the wilds of the airport strip. And while it's unusual to see any of the prospective buyers in full black tie (as in days of yore), the sale is scarcely casual. Prices have risen sharply in recent years, with a top filly last season reaching $475,000. But many famous horses have been picked up for a virtual song, and it's this possibility, even now, that packs the bidders in. Nijinsky, for example, sold for $84,000 in 1969, and went on to win nearly $700,000 in prize money before reaping another fortune in stud fees. In 1977, Glorious Song brought only $36,000. Her owner subsequently sold half-shares for $500,000 and $1 million; her lifetime earnings of $1,004,534 set a record for Canadian-bred horses.

For most people who aren't born into the world of racing, the Woodbine sale's real interest lies not in the horses, most of which are reserved, dignified and quite beautiful, but in the bidders, who project entirely opposite qualities. On each of the sale's three nights, they can be seen with noses buried in thick catalogues, like opera buffs deep in contemplation of the program. For each "hip number" or lot of merchandise, they pretend to skim a somewhat laborious outline of the horse's first, second, third and fourth dam, along with precise accounts of each ancestor's or relative's earning power. But this is strictly for show. A serious bidder will have committed all the data to memory well beforehand; he'll also have hired an independent veterinarian to give the animal an exhaustive examination and may have engaged one of Toronto's three "blood-agents" to appraise the horse's potential, or retained a blood-agent to bid for him by proxy.

This is a not uncommon act of subterfuge. Generally speaking, all the buyers know one another, all the way back to *their* third and fourth dams. But many are reluctant to make their business known — although some like to be seen bidding for reputation's sake. A few prefer to lurk at the back of the arena, out of sight of their competitors — so a bid-spotter has to be stationed there, connected by microphone to the auctioneer. This used to be a favourite device of E.P. Taylor, the noted industrialist and proud owner of Windfields Farm, the Oshawa breeding concern that still supplies one-sixth of the yearlings at the sale.

Once the bidding starts, it usually mounts in brisk thousand-dollar increments. The auctioneer first determines the opening figure, which is frequently a vendor's reserve. (In the past, some horses went for as little as $2,000, in contests lasting only a matter of seconds, but the majority today are knocked down in the $20,000 to $40,000 range.) People signal their bids with a weird assortment of hand gestures, finger movements, ear-scratchings and eyebrow-raisings that recall a roomful of sufferers from mild cases of St. Vitus's Dance. In fact, one twitchy matron was reprimanded by the auctioneer not long ago for blowing her nose at the height of the bidding. This was interpreted as a bona fide bid, and threw the whole process nicely out of whack.

It's altogether an odd, somewhat anachronistic spectacle: ancient rite of the colourful tribe of Anglos who long dominated the region; the perfect subject for a savagely satirical cartoon. And though it *seems* at variance with our other markets, nothing could in fact be more definitive; because plain old horse-trading, after all, is what it's ALL about.

Harrison's Fisheries,
Prince Edward County

*People have gathered at the mouth of the Bay of Quinte
to trade in fish since the time of Indian settlements. Now
the area's one hundred and six commercial fishermen
bring their catch to Harrison's to be packaged for shipment
to North American markets or frozen for export overseas*

Harrison's Fisheries

SUSPECT EELS AND UNLUCKY KEELS

PRINCE EDWARD COUNTY to the east of Picton juts out into Lake Ontario, set apart from the "mainland" in outlook and history. Its towns and villages are very old, dating from the exodus of United Empire Loyalists, Methodists and Quakers.

Harrison's Foods Ltd. (the corporate name of the place locals refer to simply as "the fish house") stands where the Bay of Quinte meets the lake. People have gathered there to trade in fish since the time of Indian settlements. Not so long ago, the Picton area's shipbuilding yards produced a number of early steamboats and graceful schooners. But now, these waters are the preserve of the area's one hundred and six commercial fishermen, who bring their catch to be packaged for shipment to North American markets or frozen for export overseas.

Harrison's does very little retail trade; primarily, it's a registered packing plant. (There are very few local outlets for fresh fish, except a couple of small vendors in Brighton and Carrying Place.) But the variety is there: perch and eel, pickerel and whitefish, bullhead, sunfish, herring and smelt. Hans Zander noticed large numbers of American eels, which spawn in salt water off the Bahamas. He was told how they make an extraordinary migration north to the St. Lawrence, entering the lake via specially constructed "eel ladders" and returning south for final spawn, if they evade the fishermen's nets. If not, they're destined for Germany, since they contain too many harmful chemicals for Canadian consumption — a sad and sobering thought. Zander also learned about a local superstition among the fishermen. It seems that Prince Edward County sailors never paint their vessels a real blue, "because it's unlucky. The only real blues you see are on yachts — and that's because yachtsmen don't know any better."

The Harbourfront Antique Market, Toronto

The market's dealers (who run the gamut from moon-lighting schoolteachers to full-time professionals with shops elsewhere) bring what they believe will sell — most often, something small enough to sway the impulse purchaser and fit in the trunk of his car

A Farm Estate Auction near Guelph

Every weekend, hundreds of city-dwellers desert apartments already overstuffed with objects plucked out of time and place, and head for the surrounding countryside, dead set on acquiring more and more of the same. A rural auction is the stamping ground of people who have no earthly use for a dough box — only a burning desire to use one as a planter

The Harbourfront Antique Market

BRASS BEDS AND FRIENDLY FEDS

HARBOURFRONT began as a somewhat idle election promise in the 1972 federal campaign, when the Trudeau Liberals announced a plan to buy up virtually all the vacant lots and derelict buildings along Toronto's downtown shoreline and transform them, fairy-godmother-like, into public parkland. The idea made a good deal of sense. Toronto grew up on lake transportation, but its docks and wharves had lost out to the railways, which took over not only their function but their physical space. The result was that residents were cut off from the lake by a maze of marshalling yards — not that the lake, with its outmoded and crumbling warehouses, offered much incentive to trespass.

After the election, however, neither Ottawa nor the city did much to follow through. For a time, Harbourfront consisted of a paved sidewalk, two pedestrians wide, that sadly meandered from York Street in the east to Bathurst in the west. But by the mid-to-late 1970s, things began looking up. The York Quay complex was attracting weekend strollers with imaginative landscaping, children's play-grounds, movie theatres, concert spaces, craft studios, art galleries and restaurants. Indeed, it proved such a success that by 1987 a $300 million expansion between Spadina and Bathurst (complete with office towers, shops and condominiums) will do much to limit the access that was supposed to be protected.

No matter. As such projects go, the whole idea was reasonably enlightened — and despite delay and (some would argue) miscalculations, the ninety-two-acre park is working fine. And, since 1977, one of its most popular attractions has been the Sunday antique market, featuring some two hundred dealers from throughout Ontario, and drawing up to fourteen thousand customers each weekend.

In summer, the market takes place outdoors at the foot of Spadina Avenue, on a site covering about two city blocks. This is by far the more pleasant location, since in winter it moves to claustrophobic quarters in a former warehouse on the north side of Queen's Quay. In either case, the organizers (a group of local dealers) charge only $25 for the smallest selling space, and admission is always free.

In the past couple of years, the T-shirt/health food/Taiwan bracelet crowd have been creeping in, and there's a constant battle to keep up the proportion of "real" antiques. The dealers (who run the gamut from moonlighting schoolteachers to full-time professionals with shops elsewhere) bring what they believe will sell — most often, something small enough to sway the impulse purchaser and fit in the trunk of his car. Glossy oak and gleaming brass, 1930s nostalgia and 1940s clothing are usually guaranteed, but no one knows what may turn up on a given day — least of all the dealers, who make a practice of picking their opponents' booths in the early hours, snatching bargains that appear elsewhere, their prices trebled, later in the afternoon.

Harbourfront isn't known for museum-quality goods — but many vendors take care to display photographs of the better pieces they're hoarding back at home. And it's a fascinating place to browse, comparison shop and learn a little bit about the past. You might even find that elusive item that's been evading you for years. Hans Zander had searched in vain for a particular sort of Victorian bird cage, all to no avail. And then one day, there it was, at Harbourfront.

A Farm Estate Auction near Guelph

*Every weekend, hundreds of city-dwellers desert apartments
already overstuffed with objects plucked out of time and
place, and head for the surrounding countryside, dead set
on acquiring more and more of the same. A rural auction
is the stamping ground of people who have no earthly use
for a dough box — only a burning desire to use one as a
planter*

A Farm Estate Auction

HOT ON THE TRAIL OF GRANDFATHER'S CLOCK

THE CLASSIFIED SECTIONS of our daily newspapers are a wonderful guide to yet another sort of marketplace. Businesses go bankrupt, and their assets go to the block: earth-moving equipment and filing cabinets, ten-ton trucks and typewriters. From the Metropolitan Toronto Police auction of lost and stolen bicycles and the Toronto Transit Commission's annual haul of mislaid umbrellas, to the lavish catalogues of Sotheby's and Phillips Ward-Price, auction fever stalks the land.

Every weekend, hundreds of city-dwellers desert apartments overstuffed with objects plucked out of time and place, and head for the surrounding countryside, dead set on acquiring more and more of the same. A rural auction is the stamping ground of people who have no earthly use for a dough box — only a burning desire to use one as a planter. They come in blue jeans and designer jackets, BMWs and old Volkswagens, to pick over the remains of someone else's life, and take it home.

The days of the 50-cent pressback chair are long gone, and any promising sale is almost certain to be thick with dealers, who know exactly what a given item is worth. They are intrigued to see the amateur, bidding twice what he'd pay in a reputable shop, caught in the grip of acquisitive frenzy. But any exurban sale is a pleasant outing — a chance to watch the local farmers in search of items they'll actually *use*, and an excuse to eat terrific sandwiches and pies, courtesy of the local church group. A genuine estate sale, held on a century farm that's been occupied by the same family for generations, becomes a painless history exercise — and, given a reputable auctioneer, a chance to buy something that comes from inside a particular house, as opposed to a shop halfway across the province.

The bargains may be few and far between, but there's always the *chance*, and it's a marvellous way to spend a Saturday afternoon. Hans Zander joined the throng one day at a sale north of Guelph, where he found an Ontario Gothic farmhouse containing a little bit of everything: a hundred years' worth of furniture in various states of disrepair, reams of clothing, bedding and blankets, broken appliances and mismatched cutlery, a wagonful of rusty iron, pictures of somebody's rather grim-looking relatives and, to top it off, a couple of unstrung violins.

The Toronto Stock Exchange

When Hans Zander gained admission to the trading floor, he found himself adrift in a sea of paper. Thousands of pieces were scattered underfoot, hundreds of telephones rang at once, and agitated men in purple, orange and green jackets bawled out orders at the top of their lungs, making frantic signs the while

The Toronto Stock Exchange

HOT PURSUIT IN THE PAPER CHASE

LOOKED AT with an unbiased economic eye, the stock market is simply a sort of auction with no upper limit on the bids. But neither do the TSE's transactions have a lower limit, as horrified traders learned in the crash that launched the great Depression, when stocks that sold one day for twenty or thirty dollars began changing hands for literal pennies. Those days are mercifully behind us. Meanwhile, the TSE continues on its way, making the words "Bay Street" synonymous with high finance, and providing a useful whipping boy for regional discontents.

The TSE began in 1852 as a loose-knit organization of traders in stocks and bonds, incorporating in 1878 by a special act of the provincial legislature. Even so, it remained totally unregulated by any authority except the consciences of individual members — and when rules *did* arrive, they weren't the result of excesses on the TSE's part, but those of another institution it subseqeuently absorbed, the Standard Stock and Mining Exchange. This dubious outfit was a hotbed of the most transparent flimflams, and managed to give Toronto its unenviable (but absolutely deserved) reputation as stock fraud heaven — a reputation it took both the TSE and the provincial government years to live down.

When the TSE first built on Bay Street (on land acquired from Sir Henry Pellatt, the czar of Casa Loma), it was generally agreed that Toronto was the less important Canadian exchange, running a distant second to Montreal. But the balance had already begun to shift, thanks largely to the mining industry. The Klondike gold rush of 1898 had made everyone suddenly desperate to take a shot at striking it rich overnight. Soon prospectors in northern Ontario were doing just that — first in the Cobalt silver boom of 1903, and later in various mini-gold-fevers. Since no law prevented them from doing so, two groups of businessmen had set up their own exchanges solely for mining shares, which merged in 1899 to form the Standard, with headquarters on Scott Street, near

King and Yonge. Until it was finally shamed out of existence, this dreadful institution managed to bilk countless thousands of dollars out of naive speculators both here and abroad.

The Standard's fly-by-night operators had a finite number of tricks, but they worked them to perfection. The basic ploy was to buy a mining claim for a song, charter a company with the (probably worthless) claim as its only asset, and get it listed on the exchange. Next they'd begin to boost the price — either by buying optimistic coverage in the financial press or launching a word-of-mouth campaign. One forward-looking villain had his desk telephone rigged to a secret button in the carpet beneath his feet. He'd receive starry-eyed investors in his offices, then excuse himself to take a totally bogus call. "The samples have assayed at *what?!*" he'd cry. "Get back to town as quick as you can, and don't breathe a word!" His victims, certain of an inside track to surefire fortune, fell with resounding thuds.

In those days, a buyer could purchase shares on ten percent margin — meaning that to buy a hundred shares of Lucky Strike Gold Mines at $10 a throw, you'd put down $100 in cash and pray that the price would shoot up, enabling you to sell enough to pay off the balance owing and reap a handsome profit on the rest. But many Standard brokers, working out of "bucket shops" or "boiler rooms," would simply pocket the customer's down payment without actually buying anything — then drive the price down (just as they'd driven it up in the first place), causing the hapless investor to forfeit his order and allowing the brokers to quietly scoop up the stocks at bargain rates. None of this sat very well with the more legitimate exchanges — but too much money was pouring in for anyone to rock the boat, so everyone merrily stayed aboard, from the 1890s till the crash of 1929.

In the first years of the Depression, Montreal's fine old brokerage houses started going belly up, but no member of the Toronto exchange actually declared bankruptcy. This underscored the fact that Toronto was becoming the more important financial base, hinting at the way capital was already moving westward. In 1934, the Standard was put out of business by provincial edict, and merged with the TSE — which in 1937 tore down its old premises and erected a new structure on the same site.

Standing today in the tiny visitor's gallery and looking down on the trading floor, not much seems to have changed. On a busy trading day the scene can still resemble a vintage film set. Hans Zander spent several afternoons perched in the gallery, and gained admittance to the floor itself (a rare privilege for any outsider), where he found himself adrift in a sea of paper. Thousands of pieces were scattered underfoot, hundreds of telephones rang at once, and agitated men in purple, orange and green jackets bawled out orders at the top of their lungs, making frantic signs the while.

What wasn't apparent to the casual observer was that, as the 80s began, financial power again drifted westward, toward Alberta. The TSE wasn't seriously threatened — but it embraced technology just in case, with something called CATS (for computer-assisted trading systems) which enabled brokers across Canada to establish instantaneous links, simply by punching the keys of a video display terminal. Tomorrow's commerce will bring futuristic techniques we can only guess at — so it's fitting that the TSE has moved to the Exchange Tower, an ultra-modern complex at the corner of King and York streets.

It remains to be seen how this will affect the financial community. Like any other market, the exchange has come to be the centre and symbol of its district, a neighbourhood every bit as distinct as Kensington. People who work there — not just brokerage employees, but financial journalists, researchers, bankers, entrepreneurs and tip sheet writers — share a common locale, stamped with their personalities. Certain restaurants, from the elegant Winston's to the humblest greasy spoon, are the scenes of far more business deals than the trading floors of other, smaller exchanges. So are the brokers' favourite barbershop (in the basement of the Bank of Nova Scotia building at King and Bay), their favourite gymnasium (the Cambridge Club) and the offices of their favourite law firms (Tory, Tory, Deslauriers & Binnington for P.C.s; Blake, Cassels & Graydon for Grits). There's even a common folklore — like the story of a cat (political allegiance unknown) that used to live in the exchange building. Mining shares were said to be ready for a jump whenever she had a litter.

Nobody knows how much the community will change when the TSE makes its move. But surely the powers that be will make efforts to preserve at least the present building's façade — a stone frieze above the main entrance that for decades has been pointed out to delighted tourists. It depicts a long line of archetypes — a pudgy businessman in top hat and morning coat, a labourer with sleeves rolled halfway up his muscular arms, and so on — each marching in step, presumably toward a Glorious Future. What no one noticed until the building was completed is that, from certain angles, the capitalist seems to have his hand in the pocket of the workingman — a nice touch that helps keep matters in perspective, here in Canada's busiest marketplace.

Three Special Auctions: autos in Oshawa, livestock in Joyceville and flowers in suburban Toronto

Ontario is full of markets the public never sees, hidden away in obscure locations, their doors open only to a professional clientele who deal in goods ranging from livestock to flowers to pre-owned automobiles

Three Special Auctions

THE OSHAWA AUTO AUCTION

THE MILLS OF GOVERNMENT intervention may grind exceeding fine, but occasionally one of their victims manages to turn his experience to the good. This was the challenge awaiting Frank Wills, whose farm was expropriated by Ontario's Big Blue Machine for the mythical Pickering airport. Undaunted, he moved east to Courtice — between Oshawa and Bowmanville — there to open an auction hall specializing in anything that moves on four wheels.

It isn't open to the public — only to registered dealers, who arrive from all across the country. Each Wednesday, five to six hundred cars come rolling down one of three lanes, depending on their model years, under sternly worded signs announcing that "police cars and cabs must be identified." Each pauses briefly on the block, commands its price, and is whisked out the door, to surface on your friendly neighbourhood lot.

Three auctioneers work all the lanes at once, producing an unholy din. But this is music to Wills's ears. He looks upon his enterprise as "a modern version of the old horse-trading centres." Twice a year he leases the building to a firm called ABC Auctions, which deals in antique vehicles. These are obviously far more desirable investments than your basic $100 as-is clunker — for example, a magnificent 1927 Packard that reached $27,700.

THE JOYCEVILLE LIVESTOCK AUCTION

Although this sale is less than twenty years old, it probably resembles in its important details the stock auctions of a century ago. Every Tuesday at 1:30 in the afternoon, anywhere from twenty-five to one hundred and fifty bidders arrive in the town of Joyceville, just to the north of Kingston on Highway 15. Some are wholesalers; others are small shopkeepers or neighbouring farmers who've made consignments to the sale. Fred Gordon, the owner and auctioneer, handles anything they care to give him, except poultry. It's a businesslike, almost formal atmosphere, broken only by Gordon's monotone as he describes each lot and accepts the bids from buyers who sit in bleachers on every side of a large viewing pen.

The Malton flower auction

This auction, held at the offices of the Ontario Flower Growers' Co-op on Mississauga's Ambler Drive, is distinguished by the serious, even ruthless approach to the purchase of delicate blossoms. The market's open from Tuesday to Friday — but the big days, the days when grown men get worked up over nasturtiums, are Tuesdays and Thursdays.

All the flowers — even the most exotic varieties — are grown in Ontario greenhouses. The market resembles tobacco exchanges, since the only sellers are the co-op's one hundred and fifty-three members, one of whom doubles as auctioneer; the buyers are retail florists and garden suppliers from as far afield as Buffalo and western Quebec. Everything that can be commercially produced in our less-than-temperate zone — bedding plants and potted plants, tropical blooms and cut flowers, small trees and seedlings — comes wheeling in by the wagonload, to the tune of $8 million-worth a year. For Hans Zander, the market provided both a riot of colour and a somewhat blessed relief — since flowers, unlike animals, are incapable of protesting their fate.

Select Bibliography

Addison, William. *English Fairs and Markets*. London: B.T. Batsford, 1953.

(Anonymous). *Historic Windsor, Ontario, Canada, A sketch of a Dynamic Canadian City*. Windsor: Rotary Club of Windsor, 1950.

(Anonymous). *The Tobacco Leaf Yesterday and Today*. Delhi: Township of Delhi Public Library, 1979.

Arthur, Eric. *Toronto, No Mean City*. Toronto: University of Toronto Press, 1964.

Bailey, T.M. and Carter, C.A. *Hamilon, Famous and Fascinating*. Hamilton: W.L. Griffin, 1972.

Barkey, Jean, editor. *Stouffville, 1877-1977*. Stouffville: Stouffville Historical Committee, 1977.

Barnett, W.E. (and others). *St. Lawrence Hall*. Toronto: Thomas Nelson, 1969.

(Baycrest Terrace Memoirs Group.) *From Our Lives: Memoirs, Life Stories, Episodes and Recollections*. Oakville: Mosaic Press, 1979.

Berchem, F.R. *The Yonge Street Story*. Toronto: McGraw-Hill Ryerson, 1977.

Berry, Brian J.L. *Geography of Market Centers and Retail Distribution*. Englewood Cliffs, New Jersey: Prentice-Hall, 1967.

Biesenthal, Linda. *To Market, To Market*. Toronto: PMA Books, 1980.

Bowen, David. *Bateman's Law of Auctions, with Forms, Precedents and Statutes*. London: The Estates Gazette, 1933.

Bruce, Harry. *The Short, Happy Walks of Max MacPherson*. Toronto: Macmillan, 1968.

Campbell, Marjorie Freeman. *A Mountain and a City: The Story of Hamilton*. Toronto: McClelland & Stewart, 1966.

Davies, Blodwen. *A String of Amber*. Vancouver: Mitchell Press, 1973.

Deutsch, Grace. *Country Fairs of Ontario*. Toronto: Totem Books, 1979.

(Editors of *Harrowsmith*.) *The Canadian Whole Food Book*. Camden East, Ontario: Camden House, 1980.

Essex County Historical Society Papers and Addresses. Various numbers.

Evans, Lois C. *Hamilton: The Story of a City.* Toronto: Ryerson Press, 1970.

Fetherling, Doug. *Gold Diggers of 1929: Canada and the Great Stock Market Crash.* Toronto: Macmillan, 1979.

Firth, Edith G. *The Town of York 1793-1815.* Toronto: University of Toronto Press, 1962.

Greenhill, Ralph. *The Face of Toronto.* Toronto: Oxford University Press, 1960.

Guillet, Edwin C. *The Pioneer Farmer and Backwoodsman.* Toronto: The Ontario Publishing Co., 1963.

Harney, Robert F. *"The New Canadians and Their Life in Toronto".* Canadian Geographical Journal, April/May 1978.

Harney, Robert F. and Harold Troper. *Immigrants: A Portrait of the Urban Experience, 1890-1930.* Toronto: Van Nostrand Reinhold, 1975.

Hart, Patricia W. *Pioneering in North York: A History of the Borough.* Toronto: General Publishing 1968.

Horst, Isaac R. *Up the Conestoga.* Mount Forest, Ontario, 1979.

Jones, Robert Leslie. *History of Agriculture in Ontario, 1613-1880.* Toronto: University of Toronto Press, 1946.

Kong, Colleen Anderson. *Canada's Capital Inside Out.* Ottawa: Waxwing Productions, 1978.

MacEwan, Grant. *Agriculture on Parade.* Toronto: Thomas Nelson, 1950.

Mika, Nick and Helma. *Toronto, Magnificent City.* Belleville: Mika Silk Screening, 1967.

Morrison, Neil F. *Garden Gateway to Canada.* Toronto: Ryerson Press, 1954.

Moyer, Bill. *Waterloo County Diary.* CHYM, Kitchener, 1970.

Mund, Vernon A. *Open Markets.* New York: Harper & Brothers, 1948.

Perry, Susan and Joe McKendy. *Ontario Country Diary.* Toronto: Nelson Canada, 1980.